Extreme Dinosaurs

by Luis V. Rey

chronicle books · san francisco

This book is once again dedicated to Carmen . . .
for her love, patience and friendship,
and to the memory of my parents.

ACKNOWLEDGMENTS

I wish to give special personal thanks (in no specific order) to Darren Naish, Tracy Ford, George Olshevsky, Scott Hartman, Greg Paul, Bob Bakker, Jacques Gauthier, Ken Carpenter, John Ostrom, Alan Gishlick, Cristiano Dal Sasso, Marco Signore, Eric Buffetaut, Sankar Chatterjee, Xu Xing, Phil Currie, Kevin Padian, Dale Russell, David Lambert, Ruben Martinez, Luis Chiappe, Mark Norell, Brooks Britt, Peter Buchholz, Brian Cooley, Don Glut, Mark Hallett, David Peters, Dan Chure, Jim Kirkland, Rene Hernandez, Don Henderson, Ralph Chapman, Mary Schweitzer, Tom Holtz, Stephen Gatesy, Charlie McGrady, Russell Hawley, Stephen and Sylvia Czerkas, Sandra Chapman, David Martill, William Blows, Angela Milner . . . and Larry Martin (for letting me wear his "Birds Are Not Dinosaurs" badge upside down!). They all have helped me and contributed in one way or another to the technicalities of putting this book together, continuously inciting me to discuss and study paleontology and at the same time produce all this artwork throughout the years.

Also my special extended thanks to John Lanzendorf, Mary Kirkaldy, Dick Peirce, the Deikes, Mark Kaplowitz, John Sloane, Charles Crumly, Byron Preiss, Howard Zimmerman, Mike Skrepnick, Mike Howgate, Martin Wilson, Ben Morgan, Jonathan Hateley, Wildlife Art, Janet Smith, Maasaki Inoue, Kaiyodo, Michael Trcic, David Krentz, William Monteleone, Steve White, Larry Felder, Maximo Salas, everybody at the Web's Dinosaur List and everybody I have met at the Society of Vertebrate Paleontology meetings and symposiums for continuous, uninterrupted inspiration. There are many more . . . but little space to thank all of them, so my apologies to anyone not mentioned.

Editor: Howard Zimmerman.
Editorial and Text Consultant: Ruth Ashby.
Book design by Gilda Hannah.
Typeset in Giovanni.
The illustrations in this book were rendered in acrylics.
Printed in Singapore.

Library of Congress Cataloging-in-Publication Data
Rey, Luis (Luis V.)
Extreme dinosaurs / by Luis V. Rey.
p. cm.
ISBN 0-8118-3086-1
1. Dinosaurs-Juvenile literature [1. Dinosaurs.]   1. Title.
QE861.5 .R49 2001   567.9—dc21
00-011898

Distributed in Canada by Raincoast Books
9050 Shaughnessy Street, Vancouver, British Columbia V6P 6E5

10 9 8 7 6 5 4 3 2 1

Chronicle Books LLC
85 Second Street, San Francisco, California 94105
www.chroniclebooks.com/Kids

CONTENTS

Introduction   6

Are Dinosaurs Alive Today?   9

Old Bones from the Old World   16

Bones on the Range—North America   22

Strange Southern Dinosaurs   28

African Dinosaurs   34

The New Chinese Revolution   38

The Weird and the Wonderful   52

Glossary   60

Index   62

Introduction

Dinosaurs haunted my childhood. When I was young, I was in awe of the immense dinosaur skeletons that towered over me in museums. I became lost in the incredible dinosaur pictures I saw in books. I drew endless numbers of dinosaurs in my school notebooks and dreamed of becoming a dinosaur artist when I grew up. Dinosaurs seemed part of a lost fantasy world that I loved returning to again and again.

But as I got older, I discovered that dinosaurs were more than just fantasy. They were science, too. The science of understanding dinosaurs is always evolving, as more fossils are found and interpreted. For paleontologists, the scientists who study ancient animals and their environments, dinosaurs are a never-ending source of fascination. Solving the mysteries of these long-lost creatures turns paleontologists into detectives on the track of the next exciting discovery. As a dinosaur artist, I can be a detective, too. I spend my time learning about evolution and reconstructing ancient life. It is my job to study fossils that have been reconstructed. Then I bring them to life in paintings, trying to be as accurate as possible.

There has never been a more exciting time to study dinosaurs. The better we get to know them, the more weird and wonderful and extreme they seem. We know a lot more about dinosaurs than we did when I was a kid. We used to think that dinosaurs were sluggish, cold blooded, and not very bright. Then in 1964, Yale paleontologist John Ostrom found the arms and claws of a two-legged meat eater he named *Deinonychus*. *Deinonychus* had enormous sickle-shaped claws on its feet. This meant that in order to kill its prey, it had to be able to leap into the air, cling to the victim with its hand claws, and slash with its feet. *Deinonychus* must have been a real acrobat. Could it be that dinosaurs were much more active than we had thought?

Other extraordinary discoveries followed. In 1978, Jack Horner found the nest eggs of the plant eater *Maiasaura* in Montana. Near the eggs were the skeletons of young *Maiasaura*—and of adult *Maiasaura*, too. Horner concluded that some dinosaurs might have cared for their young after they hatched, much like birds nesting in colonies. This was quite a surprise! Suddenly dinosaurs were even more popular. Scientists searched the globe looking for new fossils.

Because of the discoveries of the past twenty years, today we know about many more dinosaurs. And we've learned

not just how their bones fit together, but what kind of skin some of them had, and how they may have looked when they were alive. For the first time, we have seen the traces of internal organs clearly imprinted in rocks.

As we learn more about them, the way we picture dinosaurs continues to change. Now we paint dinosaur skin as striped or mottled, brightly colored for display, or dark and dull to blend into the landscape. Some of the giant plant-eating sauropods are ornamented with armor plates and spikes, some of the small meat-eating theropods are shown with feathers. Although we still know very little about how dinosaurs looked on the out side, we are learning fast. Some long-familiar creatures may turn out to have been super-strange. I can't wait to draw them.

I'm thrilled to be living in a time of such explosive discovery. For the rest of my life, I plan to devote my energies and imagination to exploring the secrets of the dinosaur—past, present, and future.

Are Dinosaurs Alive Today?

Dinosaurs lived for 160 million years and then disappeared forever. All we have left today are their fossils. Here's how fossils were created: When dinosaurs died, their bodies usually decayed and slowly disappeared. Sometimes, though, they were quickly buried by sand or earth or in the bottom of a river bed. Then, instead of decaying, the bones were gradually replaced with minerals over the course of millions of years. When the process was complete, the bones had turned completely to stone. These are called fossils.

Fossils provide clues for most of the questions we ask about dinosaurs. Were they warm blooded or cold blooded? Fast moving or slow moving? Stupid or smart? The more fossils we find, the more answers we have—and the more questions. Our most recent discoveries have led to the most amazing question of all: Are dinosaurs still alive today? Did they evolve into birds?

The similarity between dinosaurs and birds was first noticed in 1861. That's when the first *Archaeopteryx* fossil was found in Germany. *Archaeopteryx* is a prehistoric bird. We know it was a bird because it had wings and feathers—but it looked like a dinosaur, too! It had the long, bony tail, three-toed claws, and pointed teeth of a reptile.

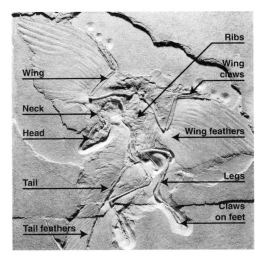

This is a photograph of the first **Archaeopteryx** *fossil that was found. Based on the wings and tail feathers, it was clearly a bird. But it also had pointy teeth and a long, bony tail. Birds don't have those, but dinosaurs do.*

The discovery caused a sensation. It seemed to support Charles Darwin's theory that animals evolved, or changed, from one species to another over millions of years. In his 1859 book, *On the Origin of Species*, Darwin had suggested that some-day we would find "missing links," animals that were connections between one species and another. Was *Archaeopteryx* the "missing link" between rep-tiles and birds? Darwin's supporter Thomas Henry Huxley thought so. He suggested that birds and dinosaurs might have a common ancestor. The two were such close relatives, he said, that *Archaeopteryx* itself might be called a feathered dinosaur!

THE ANCESTOR of modern birds might have looked something like the painting of *Protoavis*, which means "first bird," on page 11. It is based on a fos-sil discovered in Texas in 1985. *Protoavis* had wing claws and tail bones, and also probably had feath-ers. If it was truly the "first bird," then it must have been an extremely primitive one.

Today, most scientists who study ancient ani-mals agree that all birds, including the first birds, descended from theropod dinosaurs. What they don't agree on is which theropods evolved into birds and when it happened. This is a mystery, since the earliest birds and birdlike theropods were alive at the same time. There must have been an even more ancient theropod that gave rise to the birds. But we haven't found any fossils of it yet.

THERE ARE two theories about how ancient dinosaurs might have evolved into birds. The first is that two-legged dinosaurs learned to fly from the ground up. If they were active, warm-blooded creatures, they may well have evolved a protective covering like feathers. They might have eaten flying insects by running and jumping to try to catch them. Perhaps those that could run and jump the best evolved stronger arm and leg muscles and real feathers to keep them warm. The arm motion they used to catch insects might have evolved into the flight stroke—the motion that birds use to fly.

OPPOSITE PAGE: **Archaeopteryx.**

RIGHT: Rey's portrait of **Protoavis.** *The chicks hatching from the eggs represent all of the birds that evolved from the first bird. However, not everyone agrees that* **Protoavis** *was related to birds. Future research may change our present picture of it.*

Mesenosaurus *evolves into a tree-climbing dinosaur. Then this animal evolves into a feathered dinosaur.*

The second theory is that dinosaurs learned to fly from the trees down. Small, agile dinosaurs able to climb trees might have leaped from one branch to another to catch food or escape danger. Maybe it was one of these dinosaurs that evolved wings.

THE PAINTINGS on these pages illustrate the "down from the trees" theory. Starting from the left, a *Mesenosaurus* evolves into a dinosaur, which then evolves into a bird. Of the six stages, the first and last are known animals. The first

one, the *Mesenosaurus*, may have been a tree-dwelling archosaur (dinosaur ancestor) that lived about 280 million years ago. The last one, *Archaeopteryx*, lived about 150 million years ago. The others are not yet known from fossils—they are the result of scientific guesses—but something *like* them probably did exist.

There must have been a whole range of birdlike dinosaurs and primitive birds covered in scales, feathers, bristles, or down. Down is a soft, pre-feather covering that many modern baby birds have. As they grow, the down is

The feathered dinosaur evolves into Archaeopteryx. *Newly discovered dinosaurs* Microraptor *and* Sinosauropteryx *fit the bill for the animals pictured above left and center.*

In 1988, my *Deinonychus Pack* was a controversial painting. Paleontologists who favored the idea of the dinosaur-bird link loved it. Others didn't. They thought dinosaur feathers were science fiction—they wanted to see scaly skin!

Lots of evidence has piled up in favor of feathers since those days. However, today I would change some details in the painting. Now, for instance, we know that *Deinonychus*'s hands folded like a bird's wings. (If you want to see how I would portray *Deinonychus* now, look at the painting on page 55.)

OPPOSITE: *Luis Rey's* Deinonychus Pack. *When he painted this, Rey gave these small, vicious dinosaurs feathers. Today, he would paint them to look even more like birds. Recent discoveries show that several small theropod dinosaurs, like* Deinonychus, *had some kind of feathery outer covering.*

replaced by feathers. Lots of dinosaurs didn't look at all like the scaly reptiles that dinosaur artists used to portray.

Instead, they might have looked like the painting of *Deinonychus*. *Deinonychus* was a theropod. And it seems certain now that one group of theropod dinosaurs, called maniraptors, evolved into birds. The dinosaurs in *Deinonychus Pack*, pictured here, are quick running and quick thinking, possibly warm blooded and definitely feathered. To catch their prey, they leap and reach out with their clawed hands. This kind of reaching motion that might have developed into the flight stroke—and changed their arms into wings!

More bizarre dinosaurs are being found all the time, all over the world. The first dinosaurs were found in Europe, the United States, and Canada. But today, China, Mongolia, Africa, and South America have become the dinosaur hunters' paradise. Let's circle the globe and see some of the most weird and wonderful creatures ever.

Old Bones from the Old World

Dinosaur fossils were first discovered in Europe in the nineteenth century. In 1842, three unusual finds were called "dinosaurs," or "terrible lizards," by English scientist Richard Owen. Their names were *Megalosaurus* ("big lizard"), *Iguanodon* ("iguana tooth"), and *Hylaeosaurus* ("lizard of the woods"). Owen knew they were a completely new kind of reptile. Nothing like them had ever been seen before!

Twenty years earlier, amateur scientist Gideon Mantell found parts of the plant eater *Iguanodon* in southern England. He spent five years trying to convince scientists he had made a revolutionary discovery. Mantell struggled to make sense of the scattered and incomplete bones. No one had ever tried to describe a dinosaur before. Imagine finding car parts scattered in a desert and trying to put them together. If you have never seen a car before, you'll make lots of mistakes! No wonder Mantell got it mostly wrong. For instance, he placed *Iguanodon*'s spike on top of the nose like a rhinoceros's horn. It is actually a thumb spike, and *Iguanodon* had one on each of its hands. But Mantell had only discovered one of them, and mistakenly thought it was a nose horn. The thumb spikes probably were used to defend against predators as well as against other *Iguanodons*.

OPPOSITE: *This is the modern view of* Iguanodon, *with its spikes on its thumbs where they belong.*

BARYONYX ("heavy claw") was the most famous British dinosaur discovered in the twentieth century. Only one skeleton of this really strange predator has been found so far. It had two-foot-long crocodilelike jaws filled with sixty-four sharp teeth. It might have used its thumb claws to scoop fish out of the water, like a grizzly bear does. It could also seize slippery fish with its jaws, and may have hunted land animals, too.

TWO OTHER dinosaurs living in Britain 125 million years ago were *Polacanthus* and *Valdoraptor*. In the painting on the opposite page, *Polacanthus* is swinging

BELOW: **Baryonyx** *was one weird-looking dinosaur.*

OPPOSITE PAGE: **Polacanthus,** *an armored plant eater, is attacked by a pack of* **Valdoraptors.**

its body and tail sideways as it is attacked by a *Valdoraptor* pack. *Polacanthus* was a heavily armored plant eater with a square skull. It may have had a small bony club at the end of its tail. *Valdoraptor* was a fierce, two-legged predator. It probably had long, grasping fingers and big claws on its feet.

This poor *Polacanthus* has met up with some nasty customers. It will be lucky if it survives the encounter.

AN INFANT *Scipionyx* was the first theropod "mummy" ever discovered. An almost complete skeleton of this baby theropod with enormous eyes was found in Italy in 1983. It was the first dinosaur to be found with fossilized internal organs that were fairly well-preserved. This tiny chick was so perfectly preserved that its intestines can be clearly seen. Special photographs have shown traces of other organs, including a liver, right inside the tiny rib cage.

OPPOSITE: *A family portrait of* Scipionyx. *Adults feed the younger chicks, while older chicks are already hunting for themselves.*

The discovery of *Scipionyx* was really exciting and important. To make sure I got the details of my painting just right, I asked the advice of the two scientists who originally described it, Cristiano Dal Sasso and Marco Signore. They helped provide me with a detailed plaster cast and magnified photographs of the fossil.

I painted the dead chick on the left of the painting right on top of life-sized photographs of the original fossil.

Bones on the Range—North America

Not long after the first dinosaur finds in Europe, a dinosaur was found in New Jersey in 1858. It was the four-legged plant eater *Hadrosaurus*. By the 1870s, dinosaurs were found in vast quantities in the western United States. The fossil race was on. Teams of fossil hunters hurried out to Colorado and Wyoming and shipped trainloads of bones back to museums in the East. Since then, the search has never stopped. By the 1990s, more dinosaurs had been discovered in the United States than anywhere else.

WHAT'S THE most famous dinosaur in the world? Everyone agrees it's *Tyrannosaurus rex*! The first "tyrant lizard king" fossil was first discovered in Montana in 1902. Since then, it has become known as the biggest, baddest predator that ever lived. It was almost twenty feet tall and more than forty feet long. Today, we know that *T. rex* wasn't actually the largest theropod. *Giganotosaurus* from South America and *Carcharodontosaurus* from Africa were at least as large, and perhaps larger. But they weren't scarier than *T. rex*!

OPPOSITE: *Everyone's favorite dinosaur,* Tyrannosaurus rex. *A herd of* Triceratops *move across the background, while pterosaurs (flying reptiles) fill the sky.*

About two dozen *T. rex* fossils have been found. The best one is about ninety-five percent complete, so we have a good idea of what *Tyrannosaurus* looked like. We've even found a specimen of skin, which was covered in small scales. This gave the skin a smoother look and feel than that of a crocodile and most other reptiles.

IN THE PAINTING *Tyrannosaurus Rex Family Life* pictured here, a mother *T. rex* feeds her young with the remains of an *Anatotitan*, one of the duck-billed dinosaurs. In the background, another *Anatotitan* runs for its life. We don't know whether *Tyrannosaurus* actually did care for its young after they hatched, but it may have. We also don't know for sure whether youngsters were covered with down, as these are, to insulate them from the heat and cold. But some scientists think this may have been the case.

To learn more about what *Tyrannosaurus*'s life may have been like, we look at today's living predators. Large predators, like lions in Africa, find food in two ways. They hunt prey, but they also scavenge the remains of already-dead animals. Most scientists agree that *Tyrannosaurus* probably did both—just as in this painting.

ANOTHER FIERCE North American predator was the *Utahraptor*. Scientists used to think that sauropods, the enormously huge four-legged plant eaters, were safe from most predators. Then

Utahraptor was discovered in Utah in 1992. This twenty-foot-long raptor is the largest of its group yet found. If it hunted in packs, it may have been able to attack and bring down even a giant plant eater.

The main killing weapons of the *Utahraptor* were its sickle-shaped hand and toe claws. Over twelve inches long and flattened like blades, they were used to slash and tear. The victim would have died from loss of blood. *Utahraptor*'s arms, like those of other raptors, were long and built somewhat like wings. The hands folded under like wings, and the arms moved in a flapping motion. The claws on the toes were designed to hold onto prey, rather like a mountaineer's hooks. But these claws could also slash through a victim's belly. In the painting on the opposite page, the victim is an *Astrodon*, a plant eater that lived in North America at the same time as *Utahraptor*.

ACROCANTHOSAURUS was also a large North American predator. This theropod dinosaur lived about 115 million years ago in what is now Utah, Texas, and Oklahoma. On page 27 it is dining on an already-dead brachiosaur. But *Acrocanthosaurus* was thirty to forty feet long, and weighed about 5,000 pounds. It was undoubtedly not just a scavenger but a fierce hunter as well.

OPPOSITE PAGE: *A pack of* Utahraptors *attack a sauropod with teeth and claws.*

BELOW: Acrocanthosaurus *means "tall spine lizard." This illustration shows why it got that name. The tall spines may have been covered with skin, forming a leathery sail along its back.*

Strange Southern Dinosaurs

Dinosaur hunting started in South America in the late 1800s. By the 1960s, lots of important finds had been made. And in the last two decades scientists have found a treasure trove of fossils there. South America is turning out to be one of the most abundant dinosaur graveyards in the world. It is also the home of some of the most bizarre dinosaurs ever found.

GIGANOTOSAURUS is the new heavyweight champion of predatory dinosaurs. It was some five feet longer and as much as two tons heavier than *Tyrannosaurus rex*. It was more lightly built than *T. rex*, however. Its jaws weren't as powerful and its teeth were smaller and more blade shaped. Even its banana-shaped brain was smaller. And it had three fingers on each hand where *T. rex* had only two.

In the *Giganotosaurus* painting on the opposite page, it is attacking a strange-looking plant eater named *Amargasaurus*. *Amargasaurus*'s spines are meant to protect it from such monsters. But it looks as if this *Amargasaurus* is doomed.

In the background roams a herd of *Argentinosaurus*. These giant plant eaters were among the biggest of all dinosaurs. Even though the famous *Seismosaurus* was probably longer, the *Argentinosaurus* stood taller and was probably quite a bit heavier. The height of its shoulder was close to thirty-five feet, and it weighed almost 100 tons. Just one *Argentinosaurus* vertebra (backbone) is almost as tall as a human being.

The whole painting is actually a fantasy, done to show these three South American dinosaurs together. In reality, millions of years separated these monsters. *Amargasaurus* lived earlier and could never have been hunted by *Giganotosaurus*.

In 1985, a most unusual kind of two-legged meat-eating dinosaur was found in Argentina: *Carnotaurus*. Its name, which means "meat-eating bull," refers to the horns that crown its head. It had a pushed-in, flat face not found in most predatory dinosaurs. Its squat snout gave it the look of a dinosaur bulldog. In the painting on this spread, two *Carnotaurus* use their horns —and their heads—in a butting contest.

Even stranger than this theropod's face and horns were its teeny-tiny arms. They were so puny they look practically useless. And each four-fingered hand had a finger that is really a spike facing backward. What could its function have possibly been?

Good skin impressions have been found with the *Carnotaurus* fossil, so we know the exact shape of the thousands of small

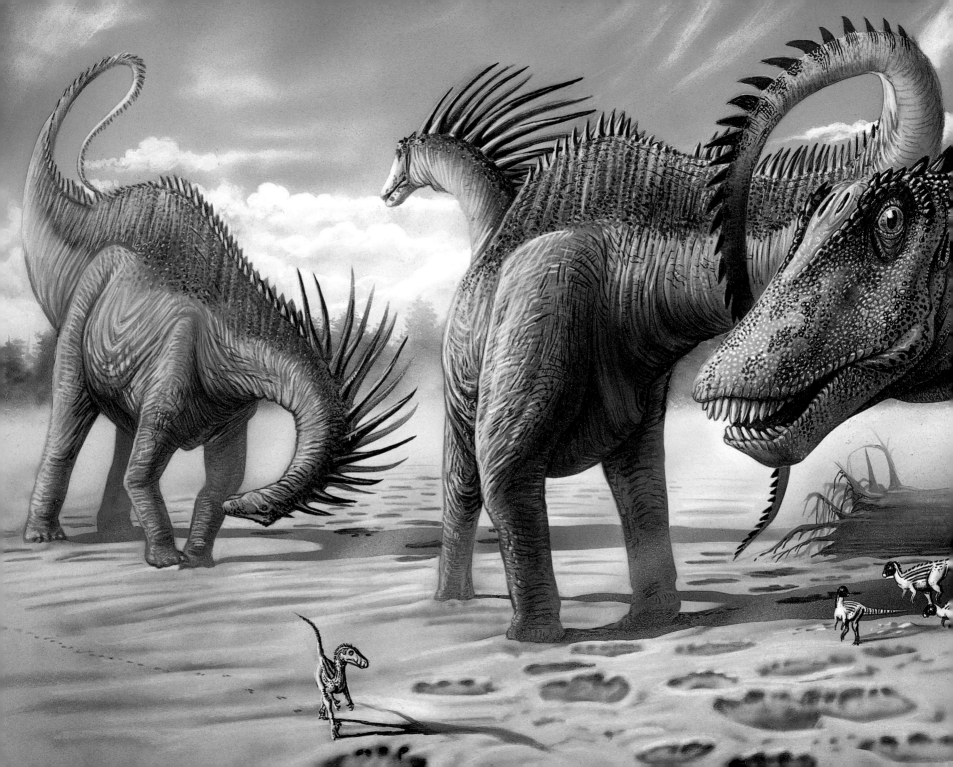

bumps—called nodules—that covered its body. As a result, we have a better idea of what *Carnotaurus* looked like than of any other meat-eating dinosaur.

AND THEN there's *Amargasaurus*—one of the weirdest-looking dinosaurs ever found. When it was discovered in the early 1990s, scientists didn't know that sauropods—the gigantic four-legged plant eaters—ever had spines. The two rows of long, curved spines on the neck and back of the *Amargasaurus* make it look like a gigantic porcupine. These spines could have been used for any number of things. Maybe they helped protect the dinosaur from predators. They could also have helped to keep it cool, especially if they were covered by a flap of skin. No one knows whether some—or all—of the spikes were covered by a sail made of skin.

In the painting on this spread, two male *Amargasaurus* use the spikes to signal to each other. No matter how we reconstruct the spikes, they must have made an awesome display!

OPPOSITE: **Amargasaurus *was not the first dinosaur discovered with tall spines on its back. But it is the only sauropod known to have had two rows of spines.***

African Dinosaurs

Fossil hunts began in Africa in the early 1900s. They have yielded some of the strangest dinosaurs ever. Digging in Africa is quite difficult. It is hard to get to many places because of the dense rain forests, and harder still to dig in places where it's wet almost the entire year. And in the north of Africa, dinosaur digs are in deserts where the temperature is over 100 degrees and there is very little water. But the efforts have been worthwhile.

CARCHARODONTOSAURUS, a spectacular discovery from the Sahara Desert, is one of the biggest meat-eating dinosaurs ever found. Only *Giganotosaurus* was bigger. *Carcharodontosaurus*'s massive skull, five-and-a-half feet long, held dozens of thin, sharp teeth shaped something like a shark's teeth. No wonder it is named "shark-toothed lizard."

The pair of *Carcharodontosaurus* pictured here are about to make a meal of a young *Aegyptosaurus*. If allowed to grow to full size, it would become a giant plant eater. This sauropod may have had a relatively short neck, and its back may have

been covered with bony armor, as were the backs of some of its close relatives. At full size it may have been huge, like *Argentinosaurus* from South America.

South American and African dinosaurs were quite similar. This means that a land link between the two continents probably existed for much of the Age of Dinosaurs.

IT'S HARD to believe that *Suchomimus* was actually a dinosaur, because *Suchomimus*'s head and snout looked very much like those of a crocodile! *Suchomimus* and crocodiles lived at the same time in Northern Africa, about 100 million years ago. But *Suchomimus* was only thirty to forty feet long. The giant crocodile was fifty feet long!

The 1997 discovery of this dinosaur in the Sahara Desert showed how extreme dinosaurs could truly be. *Suchomimus* was a powerful animal, with stout arms, huge claws, and a tall ridge along its back. Its skull, like that of *Baryonyx*, was adapted for fishing. Its long snout had about 100 pointy teeth. They were long and slender, perfect for catching and holding onto slippery fish.

Back then, the Sahara Desert wasn't a desert at all. It had lakes full of gigantic fish and lush vegetation. *Suchomimus*, crocodiles, and pterosaurs—the flying reptiles—would all have competed for the same prey.

Surprised while fishing, weird-looking Suchomimus *is attacked by a giant crocodile.*

The New Chinese Revolution

Fossil beds in China are some of the largest and most important in the world. Throughout the twentieth century, many new dinosaurs have been discovered there. In the late 1990s, scientists made some of the most surprising finds ever.

THE MOST RECENT debate about dinosaurs with feathers started with the incredible discovery of *Sinosauropteryx* in China in 1996. This three-foot-long dinosaur was about the size of a turkey and had a long reptilian tail. Its fossils, dating from 120 million years ago, are extremely well preserved. Trained experts can make out patches of skin, a faint stomach (with a mammal's jawbone in it!) and possibly even traces of eggs.

But their most amazing feature is a mane of hair or feathers that runs along the animal's back and tail. In 1996, scientists had never seen anything like it before. Was the mane actually primitive feathers?

The discovery of three *Sinosauropteryx* fossils confirmed that the covering existed—and that it was all over the animal, like fur on a

After *Sinosauropteryx* was discovered, I couldn't wait to see the fossil myself. I peered at the photographs that were published. The close-up view convinced me that the strange structures along its back were hairlike primitive feathers. In the first specimen I saw, the hand was not well preserved. So at first I reconstructed the animal with two fingers. But things change fast in paleontology! Another specimen showed us that *Sinosauropteryx* had three fingers, with a larger "thumb." So that's what you see in my painting here.

OPPOSITE PAGE: *On the left is a photograph of the actual* Sinosauropteryx *fossil. Next to it is Luis Rey's painting of how it might have looked soon after death, and while still alive (inset).*

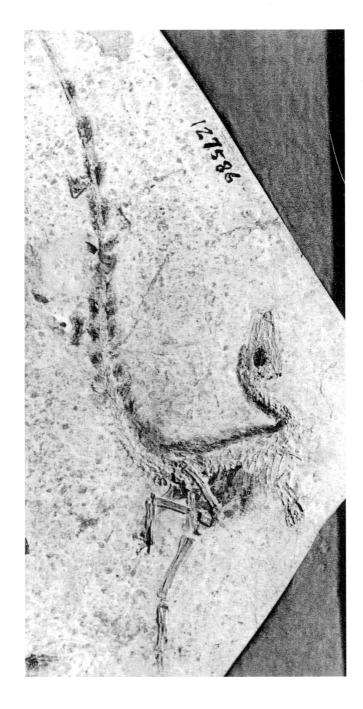

cat. No, it was not feathers of the kind that birds have. The bristly frill found running down the dinosaur's back turned out to be full-body insulation. But parts of the hairlike structures were actually hollow and sometimes branched at the tips—just like feathers.

The discovery of the *Sinosauropteryx* was revolutionary. But it was just the beginning!

THE PAINTING called *The New Chinese Revolution*, pictured here, puts many of the most exciting Chinese discoveries together. Not all of these animals lived at the same time. But by viewing them side by side, we can see the full range of theropod-to-bird evolution.

The largest of the dinosaurs in the painting is *Beipiaosaurus*, a Chinese therizinosaur. It was a plant-eating theropod that lived about 115 million years ago. This was one freaky dinosaur. With its small head, long neck, and bristled covering, it looks like a cross between a weird giraffe, a goose, and an extinct giant ground sloth. The fossils have a bristly insulation over their bodies and feathers sprouting from the arms.

The *Beipiaosaurus* are using their claws to protect themselves from a pack of dromaeosaurs. Dromaeosaurs were vicious two-legged meat-eating theropods with grasping hands and a large claw on each foot. Very likely, they were also covered with featherlike insulation.

OPPOSITE: *All of the animals pictured here are recently discovered Chinese dinosaurs.*

THIS PAGE: *Left:* Beipaiosaurus. *Above top:* Confuciusornis. *Above bottom:* Sinosauropteryx.

OPPOSITE PAGE: Caudipteryx.

In the foreground of the painting, a band of frightened *Sinosauropteryx* runs in panic, while a pair of *Caudipteryx* try to defend their nest. *Caudipteryx*, a three-foot-long theropod with long feathers on its arms and tail, looks almost like a bird. It even has the beak of a bird, except for a few peglike teeth in the front. It is the first dinosaur to be found with fully developed feathers like those of true birds. But it could not actually fly. Its feathers were the wrong shape and its arms were too small. Some scientists think it came from a dinosaur ancestor that had evolved in a birdlike direction. But others think it came from a flying bird that evolved to give up flight and became a ground animal again. At this point, no one is certain.

Perched in the trees is the primitive bird *Confuciusornis*. It had a mix of birdlike and reptilian features. It had a beak with no teeth, like a bird. But it also had long, sharp claws on its wings. The perfectly preserved *Confuciusornis* fossil shows that what we believe were males had dramatically long sets of twin tail feathers. These might have been used as a display device to attract a mate, like a peacock's tail feathers.

Seen all together, these recent Chinese discoveries prove that many small and mid-sized dinosaurs were covered with feathers, bristles, and fuzz—and not scales at all!

THE NEWLY discovered Chinese plant eater *Charonosaurus* is a member of the group called lambeosaurs. It looks very much like its North American cousin, *Parasaurolophus*, but was almost one-and-a-half times the size. It was about forty-two feet long from its snout to the end of its tail. Fully grown, this dinosaur would have weighed at least seven tons (14,000 pounds)! It usually walked on all four legs, but could also run on just its longer, more powerful hind legs.

The head crest of *Charonosaurus* was a long, hollow tube of bone. The hollow tube formed an air chamber. *Charonosaurus* could have vibrated the air inside it, which would probably have sounded like a bass trombone. This call could have been used in several ways: to let other dinosaurs know it was there, to send an alarm call to other dinosaurs when it spotted danger, and to attract a mate.

A few years ago, dinosaur scientist David Weishampel actually built a copy of the lambeosaur's hollow crest. He used plastic tubing called PVC. Then he taught himself how to play the tall, curved tube. The sounds it makes are quite low in register. Low-pitched sounds can travel for many miles. They are similar to sounds that we know some whales and adult elephants can make.

ON THIS PAGE is *Therizinosaurus*, pictured with zebra stripes. One of the reasons *Therizinosaurus* is so mysterious is that only a few pieces of its skeleton—including a gigantic hand claw—have been found so far. These three-foot-long claws, the longest of any known animal, may have been used as deadly weapons. Or they could have been used to cut down juicy leaves from high tree branches. Or they might even have been used to tear apart ant colonies or termite mounds. Aside from plants, we don't really know what *Therizinosaurus* ate.

These *Therizinosaurus* are being attacked by a *Tarbosaurus*, which was the Asian cousin of *Tyrannosaurus rex*. *Tarbosaurus* looked almost the same as *T. rex*, although it may not have been as stocky. The small, scurrying dinosaurs are *Avimimus*. They were birdlike theropods with long legs, short beaks, and wings. In the painting, these meat eaters are eager to steal a meal from the body of the dinosaur killed by the *Tarbosaurus*.

THE PAINTING on page 47 reconstructs the only known dinosaur battle frozen in time. It is based on a spectacular discovery made in Mongolia in 1971. Two dinosaurs had been buried in a sandslide—in the middle of a battle! The plant-eating *Protoceratops* has caught *Velociraptor*, a meat eater, in its powerful beak. At the same time, the *Velociraptor* is slashing through the *Protoceratop*'s belly. It is a great example of how a predator was sometimes killed by its prey.

Velociraptor, a theropod dinosaur, had agility, intelligence, and speed. The deadly sickle claws on its feet were matched by slightly smaller ones on its hands. There are good reasons to think this dinosaur had feathers. As to what color this—or any—dinosaur was, all we can do is guess.

Protoceratops had a powerful beak for biting through tough plants and an enormous head frill. Because the bony frill had large holes, it was probably used more for display to attract a mate than for defense. *Protoceratops* was also agile and was probably a ferocious defender when attacked.

At six to seven feet long, these two animals were roughly the same length. In terms of living animals, it was like a battle between a giant jackal and a giant warthog. And it proved deadly for both of them.

RIGHT: *A* **Velociraptor** *in a death struggle with a* **Protoceratops**. *Their fossils show that they were still fighting when a sudden disaster killed them both.*

ANOTHER DINOSAUR scene buried in time required real detective work to unlock its secrets. The hero here is *Oviraptor* (left), which lived about seventy-five million years ago. The fossils were found in what is now the Gobi Desert in Mongolia.

About six feet long, *Oviraptor* was a theropod dinosaur with a weird, beaked head and a helmetlike crest. The crest was hollow and filled with thin bony passageways. *Oviraptor* had only two small teeth, which has led many to wonder about its feeding habits. Today experts agree that it probably ate everything from plants to eggs to shellfish and meat. The hands were heavily clawed and folded like those of a *Velociraptor*.

Oviraptor got its name, "egg thief," by mistake. In 1923, an *Oviraptor* fossil was found near a nest filled with fossil eggs. These eggs were thought to be those of a *Protoceratops*. Paleontologist thought the *Oviraptor* had been eating the eggs. But surprise, surprise! A new expedition found an *Oviraptor* embryo inside an identical egg, proving that these weren't *Protoceratops* eggs after all.

An even more dramatic discovery followed. Researchers found a fossilized *Oviraptor* embracing at least twenty of its own eggs. With its arms outstretched, it was protecting its nest. *Oviraptor* is now thought of as a "good mother" dinosaur. It was not stealing *Protoceratops* eggs. It was just trying to take care of its own.

Why were the *Oviraptor* and its eggs buried so quickly? The painting on page 48 shows one possibility. There is a sudden sandstorm looming in the background. In a few minutes this sandstorm will bear down on the *Oviraptor* and its nest and bury them.

The painting on this page shows a second way this might have happened. A storm is brewing in the hills. Soon the pouring rain will cause a landslide that will engulf the *Oviraptor* as it tries to protect its nest.

OPPOSITE PAGE: **Death by sandstorm.**
RIGHT: **Death by landslide or flood.**

49

Finally, in the painting on page 51, *Oviraptor* eggs have survived storms, landslides, and predators to eventually hatch. Even now, the chicks won't necessarily survive to adulthood. Just as with modern birds, some chicks managed to be well fed while others starved and died. The helpless chicks remained in the nest for protection (but not for long, since they grew really fast).

How did these infant dinosaurs get fed? We're not sure, but we can guess. The mother or father *Oviraptor* may have brought food back to the nest. It would have eaten first, then forced some of the half-digested food back up from its stomach for the babies. As the babies grew, their beaks and stomach got stronger. Then the parent could have brought them chunks of a kill for the young dinosaurs to eat themselves.

Or perhaps *Oviraptor* chicks may have left their nests soon after hatching and started hunting on their own. Unless we find more evidence of hatched chicks in a nest we may never know for sure.

The Weird and the Wonderful

We have known about *Psittacosaurus* since its first discovery in Mongolia in 1923. Its name, "parrot-lizard," comes from its short head and parrotlike beak. This six-foot-long plant eater could have walked on either two or four legs. But when it was escaping from predators, it probably ran on its longer hind legs as fast as possible.

Look at the *Psittacosaurus* painting on page 53. It gives a new look to this dinosaur we thought we knew. The painting is based on fossils still being studied, so at this point it is guesswork. Perhaps it will prove to be correct, but perhaps not. We do know that the stomachs of some *Psittacosaurus* have been found to contain animal bones. So it may have been a scavenger as well as a plant eater, just like the African porcupine of today.

Here it is being chased by a hungry *Byronosaurus*. These theropods are shown covered in primitive feathers like those found on their close relatives. But this, too, is guesswork on the part of the artist. If *Byronosaurus* did have feathers they may have been bright green, as pictured here, but of course we'll never know for sure.

THE DINOSAUR in *Deinonychus: A New Look for the Year 2000* on page 55 is unlike any *Deinonychus* represented before. To some people it may look more like a turkey, or perhaps a vulture. But today we know that *Deinonychus*'s hands and arms folded pretty much like a bird's wings. This animal probably looked a lot more like a bird than we used to imagine, especially since we now think that many of the smaller theropod dinosaurs had either feathers or some other kind of outer covering.

WE ALREADY KNOW that dinosaurs may have looked completely different than we expected. They might have acted quite differently, too. Theropods, especially some of the smaller, deadlier hunters like the raptors, were more active and intelligent than we used to think.

The sketch above and the painting opposite show Deinonychus **as more birdlike than ever before.**

The painting on page 56 was inspired by a scene in a dinosaur novel, *Raptor Red*, by scientist Robert Bakker. Does a dinosaur novel sound strange? It shouldn't. After all, there are stories about dogs, cats, and horses—why not dinosaurs? The book's heroes, a *Utahraptor* family, are caught in a raging flood and are trying to escape by climbing a tree. Many people have wondered whether raptors could actually climb. Here the *Utahraptors* are forced to try, and they cling to the branches with the claws on their hands. The sickle claws on their feet act as hooks to keep them from falling off.

In such a desperate situation, the *Utahraptors* come face to face with animals they usually never meet. Here Raptor Red shares a perch with another *Utahraptor*. Together they gaze down at the bodies of the dinosaurs drowned in the flood, floating in the swirling water.

The painting on page 59 illustrates another scene from the book. Here the *Utahraptors* are having fun in the snow, much like playful animals today. They are joined by a *Troodon*, possibly the smartest dinosaur ever. (It had a bigger brain for its body size than just about any other dinosaur.) It might seem odd to see dinosaurs in the snow. But by the end of the Age of Dinosaurs, there may well have been occasional snow in the northern and southern parts of the world. And we know that dinosaurs lived there, since their fossils have been found on every continent, including Antarctica. Like other animals that survive in cold weather, these dinosaurs may have found it exciting to play in the snow!

It's fun to imagine dinosaurs as real animals, doing real animal things. The new information we've learned about dinosaurs during the past thirty years has been surprising and sometimes unbelievable. Each new dinosaur find may confirm what we know about dinosaur appearance or behavior—or turn that completely upside down. Judging by the strange discoveries of the past few years, in the future our vision of dinosaurs is going to get wilder and weirder. Weirder, more wonderful, and ever closer to the truth.

I wanted to see what a feathered dinosaur would look like in three dimensions. So I asked sculptor Charlie McGrady if we could collaborate on creating a *Velociraptor* that looks the way we now think they did. We spent many hours creating this full-sized feathered theropod. I used the same colors—blue head, white body feathers, black head feathers—that I used in my 1988 painting (on page 47). The result is a thoroughly modern version of *Velociraptor*!

GLOSSARY

Acrocanthosaurus (ack-roe-kan-tha-SAW-rus): A theropod from the Early Cretaceous period.

Aegyptosaurus (ee-jip-toh-SAW-rus): A sauropod from the Late Cretaceous period.

Amargasaurus (a-MAR-ga-SAW-rus): A sauropod from the Early Cretaceous period.

Anatotitan (an-at-oh-TIE-tan): A hadrosaur from the Late Cretaceous period.

Archaeopteryx (ar-kee-OP-ter-iks): An early bird from the Late Jurassic period.

Argentinosaurus (ar-gen-TEE-no-SAW-rus): A sauropod from the Early Cretaceous period.

Astrodon (AS-troh-don): A sauropod from the Early Cretaceous period.

Avimimus (av-EE-MY-mus): A small theropod from the Middle Cretaceous.

Baryonyx (bar-ee-ON-iks): A theropod from the Middle Cretaceous period.

Beipiaosaurus (bi-pay-uh-SAW-rus): A large theropod from the Middle Cretaceous period.

brachiosaur (BRACK-ee-uh-SAWR): one of a group of giant sauropod plant eaters.

Byronosaurus (by-RON-uh-SAW-rus): A theropod from the Middle Cretaceous period.

Carcharodontosaurus (kar-char-oh-don-toh-SAW-rus): A theropod from the Middle to Late Cretaceous period.

Carnotaurus (kar-noh-TORE-us): A theropod from the Late Cretaceous period.

carnivore (CAR-ni-vor): A meat eater.

Caudipteryx (caw-DIP-ter-icks): A theropod from the Middle Cretaceous period.

Charonosaurus (Ka-RON-uh-SAW-rus): A two-legged plant eater from the Early Cretaceous period.

Confuciusornis (con-few-shus-ORN-is): A primitive bird from the Early Cretaceous period.

Cretaceous period (kree-TAY-shus): 144 million years ago to 65 million years ago.

Deinonychus (de-NON-ih-kus): A theropod from the Middle Cretaceous period.

dromaeosaur (dro-MAY-uh-SAWR): A group of vicious theropod dinosaurs.

Giganotosaurus (gee-gan-OH-tuh-SAW-rus): A theropod from the Middle Cretaceous period.

Hadrosaurus (HAD-ruh-SAW-rus): A hadrosaur from the Late Cretaceous period.

Hylaeosaurus (HIGH-lee-oh-SAW-rus): An ankylosaur from the Early Cretaceous period.

Iguanodon (ig-WHA-noh-don): A two-legged plant eater from the Early Cretaceous period.

Jurassic period (jur-ASS-ick): 205 million years ago to 144 million years ago.

lambeosaurs (LAM-bee-uh-sawr): a group of crested duck-billed plant eaters from the Late Cretaceous period.

Maiasura (MY-ah-SORE-uh): A hadrosaur from the Late Cretaceous period.

maniraptors (man-ih-rap-tors): A group of theropods, one of which may be the ancestor of birds.

Megalosaurus (MEG-ah-loh-SAW-rus): A theropod from the Middle Jurassic period.

Mesenosaurus (meh-SEN-uh-SAW-rus): An archosaur (dinosaur ancestor) from the Early Triassic period.

Microraptor (MY-crow-rap-tor): A small theropod from the Middle Cretaceous period.

Oviraptor (OV-ih-RAP-tor): A theropod from the Late Cretaceous period.

Parasaurolophus (par-a-SORE-oh-LOAF-us): A hadrosaur from the Late Cretaceous period.

Polacanthus (POL-a-KAN-thus): A plant eater from the Early Cretaceous period.

Protoavis (PRO-toe-ay-vis): Fossil of either a Middle Cretaceous dinosaur or early bird.

Protoceratops (pro-toh-SERRA-tops): A plant eater from the Late Cretaceous period.

Psittacosaurus (sit-uh-co-SAW-rus): An herbivore from the

Middle Cretaceous period.

pterosaur (TERR-uh-sore): A flying reptile.

raptor (RAP-tor): Name given to any member of a specific group of small-to-midsize theropods.

sauropod (SAWR-uh-pod): A group of long-necked plant eaters.

Scipionyx (skip-ee-ON-icks): A theropod from the Middle Cretaceous period.

Seismosaurus (SIZE-muh-SAW-rus): A sauropod from the Late Jurassic period.

Sinosauropteryx (SIGH-no-sawr-OP-ter-icks): A theropod from the Middle Cretaceous period.

Suchomimus (soo-koh-MY-mus): A theropod from the Middle Cretaceous period.

Tarbosaurus (TAR-boh-SAW-rus): A carnivore from the Late Cretaceous period.

theropod (THER-uh-pod): One of a group of two-legged meat eaters.

therizinosaur (ther-ih-ZINE-oh-SAWR): One of a group of theropods from the Late Cretaceous period.

Therizinosaurus (ther-ih-ZINE-oh-SAW-rus): A theropod from the Late Cretaceous period.

Triassic period (try-ASS-ick): 248 million years ago to 205 million years ago.

Triceratops (tri-SER-uh-tops): A three-horned [plant eater from the Middle-to-Late Cretaceous period.

Troodon (TROH-uh-don): A theropod from the Late Cretaceous period.

Tyrannosaurus rex (tie-RAN-uh-SAW-rus REKS): A theropod from the Late Cretaceous period.

Utahraptor (YOO-tah-RAP-tor): A theropod from the Late Jurassic period.

Valdoraptor (VAL-doh-RAP-tor): A theropod from the Early Cretaceous period.

Velociraptor (vel-AH-si-RAP-tor): A theropod from the Late Cretaceous period.

Dinosaur Time Line

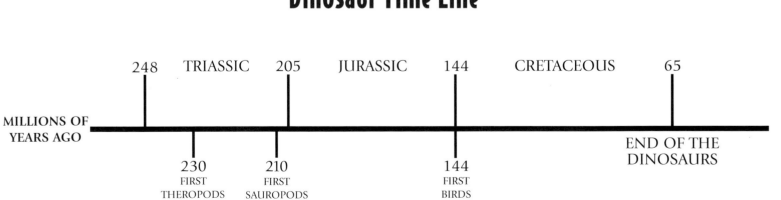

248   TRIASSIC   205   JURASSIC   144   CRETACEOUS   65

MILLIONS OF YEARS AGO

END OF THE DINOSAURS

230 FIRST THEROPODS

210 FIRST SAUROPODS

144 FIRST BIRDS

INDEX

Acrocanthosaurus, 27
Aegyptosaurus, 34–35
Africa, dinosaur discoveries in, 34–37
Amargasaurus, 28–29, 32–33
Anatotitan, 24–25
Antarctica, dinosaur discoveries in, 57
Archaeopteryx, 9, 10, 13
Argentina, dinosaur discoveries in, 28–33
Argentinosaurus, 28–30, 37
Armored dinosaurs. See Hylaeosaurus; Polacanthus
Asia, dinosaur discoveries in, 38–51
Astrodon, 26–27
Avimimus, 46

Bakker, Robert, 57
Baryonyx, 18, 37
Beipiaosaurus, 40–42
Birds. See also Archaeopteryx; Confuciusornis
  ancestors of, 10–11
  as dinosaurs, 9, 10–11
brachiosaur, 27
Byronosaurus, 52–53

Carcharodontosaurus, 22, 34–35
Carnotaurus, 30–31, 33
Caudipteryx, 8, 40–43
Ceratopsian dinosaurs. See Protoceratops; Psittacosaurus; Triceratops
Charonosaurus, 44–45
China, dinosaur discoveries in, 38–51
Colorado, dinosaur discoveries in, 22
Confuciusornis, 40–43
Crocodiles, 36–37

Dal Sasso, Cristiano, 21
Darwin, Charles, 10
Deinonychus: A New Look for the Year 2000, 54–55
Deinonychus, 7, 14–15, 54–55, 58–59
Deinonychus Pack, 14–15
Dinosaur art, 6–7

Dinosaur "mummy," 21
Dinosaurs
  birds as, 9, 10–11
  early discoveries of, 16
  feathered, 12–15
  fossils of, 9
  internal organs of, 21
  in paleontology, 6–8
  visualizing, 58
  worldwide distribution of, 14
Down, on dinosaurs, 13–14
Dromaeosaurs, 24–25, 40–42. See also Deinonychus; Microraptor; Utahraptor

Eggs, 7, 38
  of Oviraptor, 48–50
England, dinosaur discoveries in, 16–21
Evolution
  dinosaurs and, 10
  of feathered dinosaurs, 12–15

Feathered dinosaurs
  from China, 38–43, 46, 48–51
  evolution of, 12–15
Fossils, dinosaurs as, 9, 22

Germany, Archaeopteryx from, 9
Giganotosaurus, 22, 28–30, 34
Gobi Desert, dinosaur discoveries in, 46–51
Great Britain. See England

Hadrosaurus, 22
Horner, Jack, 7
Horns, of Carnotaurus, 30–31
Hylaeosaurus, 16

Iguanodon, 16–17
Internal organs, 21, 38
Italy, Scipionyx from, 20–21

lambeosaurs, 44
Landslides, 48–50

Maiasaura, 7
Mantell, Gideon, 16
McGrady, Charlie, 58
Megalosaurus, 16
Mesenosaurus, 12–13
Microraptor, 13
Mongolia, dinosaur discoveries in, 46–51, 52–53
Montana, dinosaur discoveries in, 22

Nests, 7
  of Oviraptor, 48–50
New Chinese Revolution, The, 40–41
New Jersey, dinosaur discoveries in, 22
North America, dinosaur discoveries in, 22–27

Oklahoma, Acrocanthosaurus from, 27
On the Origin of Species (Darwin), 10
Ornithopod dinosaurs. See Anatotitan; Charonosaurus; Hadrosaurus; Iguanodon; Maiasaura; Parasaurolophus; Tenontosaurus
Ostrom, John, 7
Oviraptor, 7, 48–51
Owen, Richard, 16

Paleontology, dinosaurs in, 6–8
Parasaurolophus, 44
Polacanthus, 18–19, 21
Protoavis, 10–11
Protoceratops, 46–49
Psittacosaurus, 52–53
Pterosaurs, 22–23, 24–25, 28–29, 34–35, 36–37

Raptor Red (Bakker), 56–57

Sahara Desert, dinosaur discoveries in, 34–37
Sandstorms, 48–50
Sauropod dinosaurs, 22, 26–27. See also Aegyptosaurus; Amargasaurus; Argentinosaurus; Astrodon; Seismosaurus
Scipionyx, 20–21

Seismosaurus, 30
Signore, Marco, 21
Sinosauropteryx, 13, 38–42
Skin, 8, 24, 38
  of Carnotaurus, 30–31, 33
South America, dinosaur discoveries in, 22, 28–33, 37
Spines, of Amargasaurus, 28–29, 32–33
Suchomimus, 36–37

Tarbosaurus, 46
Texas, Acrocanthosaurus from, 27
Therizinosaurs, 40–42. See also Beipiaosaurus; Therizinosaurus
Therizinosaurus, 46
Theropod dinosaurs, birds as, 10–11. See also Acrocanthosaurus; Avimimus; Baryonyx; Beipiaosaurus; Byronosaurus; Carcharodontosaurus; Carnotaurus; Caudipteryx; Deinonychus; Giganotosaurus; Megalosaurus; Microraptor; Oviraptor; Scipionyx; Sinosauropteryx; Suchomimus; Tarbosaurus; Therizinosaurus; Troodon; Tyrannosaurus rex; Utahraptor; Valdoraptor; Velociraptor
Triceratops, 22–23
Troodon, 56–57
Tyrannosaurus rex, 22–25, 28, 46
Tyrannosaurus Rex Family Life, 24–25

United States, dinosaur discoveries in, 22–27
Utah, dinosaur discoveries in, 24, 26–27
Utahraptor, 24, 26–27, 56–57

Valdoraptor, 18–19, 21
Velociraptor, 46–48, 58–60

Wyoming, dinosaur discoveries in, 22